Contemplating the

CAMINO

~ An Ignatian Guide ~

Brendan McManus SJ

First published in 2019 by Messenger Publications

ISBN 978 1 78812 078 4

Designed by Messenger Publications Design Department
Photographs provided by author
Camino Map © Alfonso de Tomas / Shutterstock
Typeset in Albertina MT Pro and Nicolas Cochin
Printed by Hussar Books

Messenger Publications,
37 Lower Leeson Street, Dublin 2
www.messenger.ie

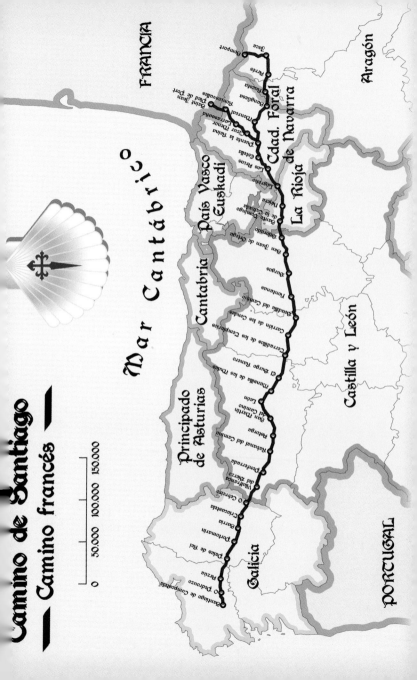

Contents

INTRODUCTION

Someone once described the Camino de Santiago as 'a very long walk'. It is a trail that goes along the road, through forests, along rivers, through mountains and eventually arrives in Santiago de Compostela, the ultimate pilgrim destination. There are a number of different routes or 'Caminos' that lead to Santiago, at least ten, and they can vary in scenery, altitude, remoteness and services along the way. Whatever route is chosen, the walker finds themselves on the road and walking for up to eight hours a day. This can initially seem arduous but finding a comfortable pace makes it much easier to sustain and ultimately enjoy. The important thing is keeping weight to a minimum and only bringing the essentials, freeing yourself from the burden of trying to bring everything (lesson #1). Interestingly, the hiker needs very little and gets along on a minimal daily budget (around twenty euro) that makes life much simpler and brings a paradoxical peace.

Something happens on the Camino that people normally only hint at or allude to: people find it good for their spirits, get perspective on difficult personal issues and can often come home transformed. The Camino is not just the physical route or trail through Spain or France, rather it is an interior issue. This is not something just for religious or people of faith; rather everyone seems to be the better for this healing of the heart, that is the Spirit of the Camino. Ironically people do all sorts of practical preparation for the Camino but neglect to do the most significant, the spiritual. Here I try to say something about what the spiritual is, how to make it accessible and explain how to tune into it more.

The founder of the Jesuits, Ignatius Loyola, was a serious pilgrim and walked the Camino trials that crisscrossed Europe in the sixteenth century. What he discovered on the road was so important that he built a walking pilgrimage into the Jesuit training (asking for food and accommodation) and the whole Jesuit system is based on travelling light and being open to the world. The heart of the Jesuit prayer is the Spiritual Exercises, a month long silent retreat of opening your heart, getting free and learning to love as Christ does. This process of becoming your true self and shedding any masks or any pretense, is exactly to what happens on the Camino and this book offers some Jesuit insights that may be of help in getting the most out of the experience.

The Ignatian system is based on a very simple insight that our experience has meaning, especially our inner moods and deeper emotions. To be able to see clearly however, we need to stand back and reflect on our journey. Seeing clearly then helps us find a direction or a path forward. It is like getting to a high point on the trail where you can see your previous journey and plan the future with great clarity. The key is getting out of our heads, away from anxiety, old patterns and fixed ideas, and moving from the ego or self-centredness to our best selves, which is what God wants. This is not as easy as it sounds though as the ego has strong defenses and resists attempts to break free from its clutches. Freedom is only possible through connecting to a higher love, and the Camino journey is the organic process of letting go of our old life or patterns and waking up to a new reality. Everything on the Camino helps this process: simple lifestyle, little technology, real conversations, lots of time alone and the slowing down that long distance walking brings.

✳ The wisdom of Ignatius Loyola, sometimes paradoxical, forms the basis of a useful guide for Camino walkers, which I have summarised here:

✳ Madness is doing the same thing over and over and hoping for different results; the Camino journey is a beautiful risk, it involves being open to a new possibility.

✳ Dissatisfaction with our normal lives is often what drives us to walk and look for more (the Camino taps your deepest desires, exposes your superficial ones).

✳ A loving presence or what we call God is continually trying to communicate with us through what happens on the road, you have to be open to listening and learning.

* Real freedom is not about escaping but rather embracing your life; finding yourself is finding God.

* Trusting in providence means letting go of the need to control and trusting that things happen for a reason (you will be tested though).

* Build in some regular time for reflecting on experience.

* Be grateful for all the good things coming your way (ingratitude is a spirit crushing way to live).

* Time spent walking alone allows things to surface within you, you come to know your truest self, but you have to break through the difficult barriers or masks you wear.

* Really challenging moments (e.g. getting lost, exhaustion, lack of sleep, injury) are where you learn the most and are what you will remember.

* For those who persevere, the Camino brings great joy and inner peace.

PACKING LIST

- A quality backpack with good waist and chest straps that sits comfortably on your hips; about 55L in size
- Walking boots or shoes (broken in)
- Plastic bags to put in stuff that must stay dry or a waterproof cover for the backpack
- 2 pair of quality hiking socks
- 2 t-shirts (not cotton)
- 2 warmer pieces of clothing: a fleece or sweater
- 2 pairs of hiking shorts
- sports underwear
- Slippers or sandals (for when not hiking)
- Raingear (jacket and trousers, or a good poncho)
- Wide brimmed Sunhat
- Sunglasses
- Flashlight and extra battery
- Sun lotion
- Lightweight camping towel
- Water bottle (at least 2Litres) or 'camelback'
- Waterproof bag for your money/camera/phone
- Eye shades
- Ear plugs

Camino
de
Santiago

Itinerario Cultural Europeo

CHAPTER 1

A Beautiful Risk:
Setting Out into the Unknown

Imagine yourself on the road in Spain: your pack is light, the weather is good, you have stopped worrying about where you will sleep, where you will eat – you are living in the moment. The spiritual aspect is letting go of all the things that normally tie you up in fear and worry (money, job, relationships, status etc.) and just being yourself. The Camino pilgrimage is an inner journey of knowing yourself, which is reflected in the outer physical journey of walking into new experiences, meeting new people and going to new places. People walk the Camino for something extra that helps them understand the ups and downs of their own lives. With the Camino, reaching a low point is something that happens to everyone at some stage. Paradoxically, this reaching of our limits is a part of a learning process. We realise who we truly are before a loving God who accepts us as we are. This experience of compassion and being unconditionally loved is transforming.

However, there is a risk in letting go, stripping off the layers of ego, pretense or hurt, and being open to a new path. Often our lives are too safe, protected and enclosed to allow us to grow or to be healed of our hurts. The Camino invitation is to move beyond the status quo, the security of the past, and into new life with the divine. What moves us is a deep desire for something more, a constant unease, or an unfulfilled heart. Often it is a profound restlessness that drives us out of our house, our comfort zone, and puts us on the road where an encounter with this personal God is possible.

CHAPTER 2

What Do You Really Want?
Preparing for the Camino

Clearly the Camino is not like a holiday but neither is it an endurance test; it is a pilgrimage of discovery and renewal, a journey into new experiences of nature, solitude, companionship and real joy. People do it for many reasons and being clear about why you are going will help you get the most out of it. Preparing yourself for the challenge of the Camino is key, understanding that you are entering a new kind of space with new rules. You have to be committed to the process of working with challenge or difficulty to see it through i.e. understanding 'you have to climb the mountain in order to get the scenic view'. Obviously there comes a point where difficulty and challenge (such as an injury) can be overwhelming, and so discretion is needed: not, for example, setting out to make things deliberately difficult for yourself (the Camino is tough enough).

Adversity is a value and an intrinsic part of the Camino, but it is not something that we create or should make more difficult for ourselves. Essentially the Camino is penitential in nature; we agree to forgo many luxuries in order to find out about our authentic selves. Often it is a sense of emptiness and dissatisfaction with our lives that propels us to try something like the Camino. Getting in touch with your real motivations for going, and daring to hope for something more, changes how you approach it. In 2011 I knew that I needed to grieve a family member and this dictated a less travelled route, my walking alone, and asking for healing on the way.

You need to prepare yourself for a great experience, anticipate some tough moments and have the flexibility to be able to roll with whatever happens e.g. injury or ecstasy. Some physical preparation is necessary but also some spiritual preparation about what do you really want:

* Why am I going?

* What am I fearful of?

* What will I enjoy, and what will be easy for me?

* Where do I need to learn?

* What can I offer to others on the way?

* What am I asking healing for?

CHAPTER 3

Being Open to the Idea that You Tread on Sacred Ground: A Journey into God

The Camino originally developed as a Catholic pilgrimage trail, an outer physical challenge of an inner process of transformation. It began around the eighth century and was popular in medieval piety as an alternative to Rome. In recent years it has seen a renaissance. Now, all sorts of people walk the trail and for many different reasons; today the Camino has a wide appeal while continuing to affect pilgrims in a mysterious and profound way.

The power of the Camino can be said to lie in two things: first, in connecting yourself to the countless pilgrims who have walked the same trail in search of meaning and redemption, and second in understanding what it is to be a pilgrim. In medieval times pilgrims would set off from their own country without money, security or maps, and walk to Santiago seeking forgiveness for their sins or an indulgence for a misspent life. The Camino has many beautiful aspects but in essence it is a penitential journey offered to God that expresses a desire to change and become a better person.

A certain amount of humility is needed to accept the fundamental starting points of the Camino: I have been created by God, I have made mistakes in my life, I want to walk this ancient path to forgiveness and true freedom. It may be unclear why you are going; many go at a time of transition or tragedy, or to intercede for another. This reason gives a tremendous meaning to the walk and all of the ancient symbols on the trail; churches, crosses, arrows and shells, suddenly take on a particular significance: I am on a journey to God. This means that everything that happens on the road, like friendships, accidents, sunrises, meals, tiredness, is part of how God is working with me.

Having some kind of reflection in your day, such as the Examen Prayer, helps to identify these moments and more importantly, how to collaborate with this loving God. Your life is transformed gradually as you walk it and live it. However, as the T-shirts in Santiago say, 'No Pain, no Glory', and the challenging aspects (pains, hunger, tiredness) are transformed if seen in this way. The Camino breaks down our defenses and allows God into our hearts if we allow it. There is a certain dying-to-self but the resurrection or rising is one of great joy.

The *Examen* (or Review of the Day) is one of the most powerful ways to discover God in our daily life. This five-step prayer helps us see the day through God's eyes:

1. Ask for God's grace.
2. Give thanks.
3. Review the day.
4. Ask for forgiveness.
5. Look forward with God.

CHAPTER 4

Real Freedom

We are all pilgrims in the world and only passing through, but it is easy to get attached to things and believe the illusion of the material world. It goes without saying that you have to let go of a lot to be a pilgrim, walking the Camino de Santiago is the modern equivalent. As on the Camino and as in life, we have to travel light and adapt to whatever comes our way whether it is the weather, health issues, unexpected obstacles or inner wounds or blocks. The point is that many of these things are beyond our control and leaving control aside and trusting in providence is the only way to really live. However, it's not so easy as it sounds as expectations get in the way like those for good food, rest, hygiene and luxury. Modern life presupposes control of our environment and lots of technology surrounds and cushions us. The liberation involved in letting go of comfort, ease and security is hard won.

Being a pilgrim on the Camino teaches this freedom from trivial 'things' to concentrate on more important ones: walking, talking, praying, appreciating, living. You actually need very little to get by and all the things we think we need (technology, comfort, riches, style etc.) has no value on the road. A rucksack that would contain everything you think you need would be impossible to carry. This is a great liberation and the recuperation of what it means to be human: a pilgrim on the road, dependent on providence and on others. The joy attached to this is palpable and infectious.

St Ignatius calls this spiritual freedom, the ability to be free of small things for greater things; things are good but only up to a point, in so far as they bring me to God. Deeper living is the desire for things that really satisfy, not empty distractions. The opposite of freedom is attachment: I can't move as I'm 'chained' to something. I have to have certain things, I impose limits. I won't accept the basic simplicity of the Camino. This is the tragedy of course, that such great joy exists so close and yet we are kept from it by smaller things.

CHAPTER 5

Trusting in Providence: Learning to Listen

Tuning into the spirit of the Camino, is learning to be a more coherent person. It means casting off the shell of self-interest to live from a deeper place by becoming more authentic, and in befriending and giving to others. Happiness is found in freely giving and receiving. This means rejecting the consumerist illusion of 'having' in favour of just 'being', seeing other people as unique creations of the Spirit and not just objects to be used. However, this is a road to be walked, as it is not easy to overcome fears, break old habits and unhealthy ways of relating. Rather it is a long and sometimes challenging process.

In the beginning there is an anxiety and a desire to control things, often manifest in bringing too much equipment, over-planning and booking accommodation way ahead. Some people spend their Camino rushing from one hostel to another, sticking to apparently rigid schedules and missing a lot of the beauty along the way. A consumerist mindset is happily often turned upside down by the vagaries of the Camino. There is often a moment of letting go, of relaxing

and of trust that is genuinely liberating. Never is it more true that 'God laughs at our plans and futile desire to control'; there is another way of walking and living that is based on trust and not fear.

However, this stepping out into the new takes courage, a desire for change and a measure of trust in providence that good things will actually happen. Often you have to arrive at some watershed moment: waking up to the madness of over-planning or of being driven by an unrealistic schedule. The Camino is the perfect stage for this spiritual change of heart; it involves daily decisions involving routes, company, food, energy and health. It invites you to be the best person you can be for that day. Learning how to listen to yourself and how to detect the inner voice of the transcendent is the challenge. We are the students and the Camino is the teacher, or rather: 'You don't walk the Camino, the Camino walks you'.

CHAPTER 6

Learning To Be Human: True Humility

Having to sleep outside in a field one night in Navarre was an experience I never wanted to have, but I survived and I learned to let go of the fear around it, a hard-won breakthrough. The pilgrim needs a certain commitment to believing in the providential process that happens along the way. Coping with the inevitable difficulties and obstacles (e.g. hunger, thirst, rain, being lost) necessitates us digging deep into our human reserves. In such an unpredictable environment mistakes are likely along the way (e.g. short temper, bad decisions, irritability) but happily, learning is the goal, not getting to perfection.

The Camino is a magical environment where every new day sees the old day wiped away in a new start. The ego and seeking to control are the common traps, as they often protect you from the very contact with humanity that is key. Wisdom, a slow interior growth, is what happens through this interaction of self, the divine, other companions and the Camino. The transformational process happens slowly and organically, and there is often an element of paradox to it, for example walking *through* obstacles to greater wisdom.

The problem is that trusting in providence means that you have to let go control and this is a costly exercise, not easily achieved. The way we have been brought up insists that you have to take charge of your life, avoid problems and insulate yourself from pain. The Camino message is exactly the opposite: you have to let go of your life and feel some of the emptiness and pain of being a limited but loved human being. You are fragile but with wonderful potential. Paradoxically, though this is very challenging and not without some fear, it does bring great joy. Being in touch with this fragile sense of humanity is a liberating truth: that we are not in control of very much.

The Camino slowly works its magic by wearing down our false defenses, by showing up our fragility, and by continually inviting us to make the jump of trust. Often it can take a whole week or even a month to achieve this, though there are no rules about when and how long.

The Camino is not about:

✳ How much of a hero you are (rather it is about being human and humble).

✳ The gear that you have bought (you need a minimum of specialist gear but experience of the divine is free).

✳ How far you walk each day (paradoxically, being injured can bring much insight).

- ❋ Keeping to a fixed plan of distance and times (God laughs at our plans or attempts to control things).

- ❋ Getting away from it all (rather, it is impossible to escape yourself on the road).

- ❋ Confirmation of your own perfection (rather, it is humanity, compassion and acceptance that emerges).

CHAPTER 7

Finding Your Own Rhythm
or Point of Balance

Camino walkers can sometimes set themselves unrealistic walking goals (I once met a man who measured his progress by how many people he passed each day). A much more helpful image is that of your own walking rhythm or pace, which though very unique for each individual, is key to walking comfortably for long distances. As a walker your job is to find this place of balance or equilibrium (your rhythm) and often it may take a while to work this out through trial and error. What are unhelpful are the extremes of over exertion or under exertion; rather there is a mid point or a zone where things work harmoniously. I learnt this through personal experience, and had to have the courage to change things that were not working e.g. avoiding too fast a pace, changing inappropriate footwear, rejecting group pressure or facing health issues.

St Ignatius has a lovely image of being at a point of balance: a free space where body, mind and spirit are in harmony.

As human beings the only way to discover this is through experience and reflection, experimenting with the limits to find what is the best fit.

As human beings we are made up of tensions and delicate balances. The experience of being pulled along too fast by others is often one of unease and discomfort, and equally being held back by dawdlers is frustrating. Pain, soreness and stiffness are the physical signs the walker has to judge well to avoid injury. There are also emotional signs such as unease, discomfort and desolation that can be equally helpful to be aware of. Obviously, these signs are not a 'head' thing but rather a body experience that we can learn to rely on. In some ways our Western education system has divorced us from our bodies and it can be a joy to relearn these basic human experiences.

CHAPTER 8

Open to Mystery and Paradox

My Camino in 2011 seemed like a pointless slog but it was only at the eleventh hour in Finisterre that I had an extraordinary release from my own grief. Having a sense of paradox is key to understanding the mystery and depth of the Camino. Paradox is not a perplexing riddle but rather a truth or insight that gradually reveals itself over time. It sometimes means staying in the emotional tension or dark places of our lives, allowing them to surface during our walk even though it can be painful and hurt more than blisters and sprains. Like a sunrise after a dark night however, this process cannot be forced but must be allowed time and space to develop and grow naturally. The beauty will gradually reveal itself through patient waiting when we least expect it.

The essence of the Camino is that there is a beautiful experience of insight, healing or re-connection awaiting you, but you have to be prepared to pass through some darkness. This could be the ugliness within yourself, a resurgence of past memories or unhealed wounds. You need to let this be transformed through the process of walking in nature and being centred and reflective even in the midst of people. There are no short cuts, easy routes, back doors. The only way is through the fragility of human reality. The paradox reveals itself when least expected, often after a 'dark night' experience of limitation and vulnerability. The resulting peace and healing is deep and enduring however. The joy of the returned and renewed pilgrim makes it all worthwhile.

CHAPTER 9

An Attitude of Gratitude

Flying home from Santiago some years ago I was delighted to be seated beside another pilgrim. Though we were complete strangers, our common Camino experience made us fast friends over the course of the flight. I was so grateful for his company during this transition back to the challenge of ordinary life. For me, the irritating part of modern consumerism is a sense of entitlement and privilege. It claims that we deserve certain things because of our wealth, status or position ('because you're worth it'). The Camino espouses the exact opposite values because it is essentially about human solidarity – that everyone is fundamentally equal and that no one gets special treatment because of who they are. Rather everyone is individual and exceptional and has something unique to offer, so everyone wins!

A key spiritual insight is seeing everyone else and everything around you as a gift. People you meet on the road are valuable in themselves and they have something to offer if you are open to receive. This means starting from a place of gratitude for everything and everyone in life that has made you who you are: spouses, siblings, friends, partners. Walking becomes an exercise in humility, recognising how lucky you are and wanting to share that generosity with others. It changes your day and fosters a new thankfulness in how you walk the Camino. This changes your heart and represents a profound challenge for the Camino walker; to accept whatever or whoever you encounter no matter how testing the personality, rough the accommodation, tasteless the food, sharp the wine. It is a very freeing thing ultimately, and invites you out from the shadow of selfishness, pride and ego. It has to be practised though, and takes a long time to master, as the demon of pride has many faces! This is the essence of the ancient pilgrim tradition, trusting in people, on their hospitality and goodwill.

CHAPTER 10

When You Reach Your Limit

In 1994 on the Camino Ignaciano (www.caminoignaciano.
org/en) I found myself going without food for a whole
day and was getting panicky and fearful. I was thinking of
packing in the whole pilgrimage as my basic necessities were
threatened (food and health). I had reached my personal
limit of uncertainty and fear, and I wanted out. With the
help of a friend I was able to turn this into a prayer (or cry)
for help. It was a most profound moment of realisation that
it doesn't depend on me, and having to pray with my fear
was ultimately liberating. From that moment on the walk
became a joy as I learned how to trust and to let go; it has
literally changed my life and my walking.

The human reality of reaching limits means being sorely
challenged and tested, but also being open to positive
change. The Camino embodies this reality par excellence;
it is a place where challenging walks, minimal facilities
and fatigue combine to create a humanising vulnerability.
Within that is a tremendous solidarity with other hikers
in the same boat. Ironically it also provides a conduit

for change, transformation and feeling alive. This is the essence of pilgrimage: a willful placing ourselves in a fluid, unpredictable situation in order to be open to the divine and the possibility for existential change. Letting go of control is another way of expressing this Camino reality, which also implies a great deal of personal freedom. It is an inner freedom to 'face the fear and do it anyway', and trust that good things exist on the other side of fear.

A spiritual practice from St Ignatius is useful here: pray with the problem. This means turning the challenging situation into a prayer and asking for help with it. There is no particular formula of words for this, rather as real prayer is being 'real with God'. It is about using your own words to express your need for help. It could be something as simple as a particular formula of words 'help me get through this', or 'help me not be so fearful, give me the courage I need to walk through this'. A similar scripture-based prayer is: 'Lord I believe, help my unbelief'. While this does not have a magical immediate effect, it does allow you to live in the reality of the situation and prayers from the heart have a way of getting heard!

CHAPTER 11

Emotions and Moods as a Way to God

Having space, simplicity and time on the way creates an interior place where emotions, memories and issues can surface. I once met a man two months on the road who confessed that he cried every day on the Camino; these were not necessarily tears of sorrow but often simply tears of gratitude, memory and forgiveness. He simply needed to create a space in his life for these emotions to surface and it was very therapeutic for him. The Camino elicits powerful feelings and emotions whether those are fears and desires, joy and delight, insecurities and old wounds, or just unexpressed energy. Getting in touch with those and finding a safe way to express them is therapeutic and necessary, as we cooperate with this healing process. It is paradoxical that this inner life of feelings and complex emotions should be so important and have such a mostly hidden influence on us. Normally we are not in touch with these in our normal lives but the Camino is a place apart.

The Camino provides a unique place where you are free

from your normal environment, roles and restrictions, and you can be yourself in all the joy, pain and messiness of that. Being out on the road, in the 'wilderness' (open to the unpredictable, beyond control or civilisation) essentially, connects us with the primitive being inside ourselves. This encourages us to let go, to be real. Spirituality teaches that getting in touch with our inner life, in all its complexity, is ultimately freeing. Sometimes the Camino can be one of the few places where there is silence, peace and simplicity; you have time to feel and to allow things to surface. It is a precious and liberating gift.

St Ignatius discovered the key role of emotions almost by chance while recuperating from a serious injury. Laid up in bed with no distractions, he noticed that there was a difference in the emotional after-effects of different kinds of daydreams. One set of fantasies about being a chivalrous hero and winning the attention of a great lady were initially stimulating but afterwards left him empty and dry. Another set of daydreams about outdoing the saints in fasting and penance left him at peace and with an enduring satisfaction. Eventually he realised that God was drawing him through the emotions and moods, away from the egocentric fantasy and towards a life lived for others. This process of separating experiences that are genuinely life giving from those that are shallow, he called discernment. In the same way the Camino invites us to discover the miracle of God working within us and drawing us towards life and love, and away from selfish distractions.

Explicitly taking time and space to reflect on life, decisions and priorities brings up these different moods and feelings, which though initially confusing, do clarify over time. Many pilgrims use a personal journal or diary to have this conversation with themselves and let feelings and issues surface.

CHAPTER 12

Trusting the Inner Voice

The Camino saved my life in 2011 when, heartbroken over the death of my brother, my walk began to focus on the healing of this wound. Totally unexpectedly, when I got to Finisterre I was able to let it all go in a cathartic burning ritual of my brother's t-shirt and reach peace. The modern world often forces us to live on the surface level (acquisition, competition, survival) while the deeper heart issues (emotions, brokenness, desire) are trivialised or ignored. Such superficial living can often cause widespread disillusionment, despair and dehumanisation. The re-emergence of the ancient Camino seeks to recover this deeper spiritual way, making reflection and silence the road to recovery. The importance of inner experience and the emotional life is widely recognised in different spiritual traditions of the East and West. The divine dwells within us as an inner voice that invites a reduced pace, a more listening attitude, and a simpler less noisy existence. The paradox is that it is in the inner work of finding yourself that you find the divine, the heart of love.

The Camino is a reflective walking pilgrimage that renovates hearts; it reunites head and heart, body and soul, spirit and humanity. It is an ancient pilgrimage path (over 1000 years old) and all the symbols, surroundings and sceneries speak of slowing down, letting things emerge and listening in the silence. Obviously very few people walk completely alone, rather we alternate between company, conversation and solitude in a very organic way. The key thing is to ensure that we have this fruitful inner silence every day, as this is the very centre of the Camino experience. It's where all the real 'heart work' gets done, and even though it can be challenging and painful at times, it is ultimately liberating and healing. The Camino is the medicine for our sick souls, a paradoxical penitential path to wholeness. This process is not something that we do or have control of; rather it is something that happens to us along the way. The most we can do is make ourselves open, and allow the source of love to touch our hearts.

CHAPTER 13

Creating Silence and Solitude

One of my enduring Camino del Norte memories is being alone high up on a ridge in the Basque country first thing in the morning. The mist was rising from the valley and I was supremely happy. One of the great Camino insights is that being alone is not lonely; rather it is a very comforting solitude. Paradoxically, it is a delight to be away from noise, conversation and distraction to be able to listen to the heart. This takes time and is very difficult in the beginning but we grow into it to the point of coming to love the silence.

The Camino, for all its focus on hostels, routes and sharing, is essentially about being alone on the road. This happens naturally as people find their own rhythm and begin to appreciate the beauty of contemplating nature. You realise that you are part of the created world, that you are created for love and from love, that life is a beautiful gift. Time alone, though initially challenging, becomes precious and paradoxically rewarding. This happens naturally as people find their own rhythm of the heart:

❋ How am I within myself?

❋ How do I feel about my life?

❋ How am I living the love within me?

❋ Where is God in my life?

❋ Where am I going?

❋ What courageous decisions to I need to take?

Deliberately taking this time to reflect and contemplate (be mindful) is precisely in order to come back to life renewed and refreshed. It is not an escape.

CHAPTER 14

From Cynicism to Hope

When I look back at previous pilgrimages, some of the difficult moments and points of giving up were the ones that turned out most fruitful. When I got a minor injury in Bilbao and had to convalesce over a weekend a Spanish priest surprised me saying that my illness was as much part of the Camino as the walking. He saw the injury as a positive thing, finding meaning in it (i.e. seeing it as a lesson in slowing down). The essence of any spiritual or heart journey is that there is a divine being providing care for and seeking communication with humanity. This is especially relevant to the Camino as it is a pilgrimage: a purposeful spiritual journey that usually has at its core some healing, release from a burden, expression of gratitude or getting insight.

The pilgrim trusts that the events and people encountered have meaning, and that the journey is leading towards some resolution, breakthrough and hope. Each person is unique and each Camino will accordingly be different, but there is normally a profound reason linking the pilgrim to the trail, not always evident to the walker. Essentially, there is negativity to be transformed, there is hurt to be healed, and there is a new life to be walked into. Accordingly, every turn of the trail can speak to the heart, every conversation has layers of meaning, and every emotion is indicating a direction or action. The meaning is often not clear initially and only becomes apparent after the event, or even after the Camino is over. The pilgrim has to live in the uncertainty of trust, believing that good will come out of it, even when it looks bleak at times. If walking the Camino teaches anything, it is that hope wins out.

CHAPTER 15

Open to Process

In 2015 I accidentally fell one morning and though I had medical attention I unwittingly walked on the injured knee for some days before giving up. It was a very testing time especially about deciding what to do, push on or pack it in? The conflicting emotions alternated between the increasing pain and the desire to keep going. Fortunately, I eventually came to the decision to quit, paying need to the body's pain message. Human beings move slowly, organically and erratically through a series of setbacks and sudden spurts. This is the paradoxical law of progress on the Camino, when you think you are ahead of the game you are not and when you feel all is lost, you have won. If there is no challenge we don't value it but also challenge in excess can get out of hand, as in my case. Sometimes pain is the warning that wakes up our understanding. However, what does complicate Camino life is our expectations. We want it all to happen now and without pain, or often our pride tells us that we are uniquely gifted in some way that will guarantee success. The Camino is a 'great leveler' in the

CAMINO CYCLE

HONEYMOON

EPIPHANY

DISILLUSION

INSIGHT

DISILLUSION

DESPAIR

sense that everyone is reduced to being a 'poor pilgrim', to coming into contact with our fragility and limits. It is only this that forces the reality onto us about the slow, gradual movement of process. If there is no struggle there is no learning.

Process means that things change according to a cycle or gradual movement. This means that we need time to go through changes, assimilate them and reflect on them before getting to a wiser place. This is about admitting that we are not gods or superheroes who can impose our will on the Camino. We find it painful to admit limits and confess to weakness, for example, being injured can be seen by some as shameful and weak. Experiencing the fullness of human experience means to live all of it, the pain and the joy, the darkness and the light. It broadens us out as people, making us capable of compassion, transcending our preoccupations and egoism, and allowing a truer sense of ourselves – that we are connected to others and the bigger world.

This diagram seeks to illustrate the pilgrim process of acquiring wisdom: it starts off with a false sense of joy (honeymoon) which begins to fade into disillusionment and then into despair – this is very difficult for people feeling that all is useless and worthless, and many want to give up at this point. There is no other way but walking through this and coming to some hard-won insights, which leads to the joy of an epiphany about the self or the world. This process does not sit still however, and we are taken into another cycle immediately. These cycles can last for one hour, one day or one month. Understanding the nature of the process means that you do not place too much stock in your surface feelings. Knowing that the way will demand everything of you makes tough days bearable, giving meaning to the experience. We are being hollowed out or divested of our 'hard shells' for a greater internal freedom and to be a more loving person. The Camino imposes its own discipline on those who choose to walk. In the words of Kahlil Gibran in The Prophet, 'Your pain is the breaking of the shell that encloses your understanding'.

CHAPTER 16

Travelling Light

A young man on a walking pilgrimage turned up with a suitcase, which his mother had packed with every eventuality in mind. Even though it had straps, it was impossible to carry and had to be ditched.

The Camino is a lesson in simplification, slowing down life, going at a slower pace and especially getting rid of unnecessary weight. There is a practical element to this in terms of reducing the weight of your backpack to make walking easier (extra weight is crucifying), but, more important, there is a whole spiritual dimension to this. Living simply, reducing mental clutter, and living in a low-tech way makes life easier (after a period of adjustment), and ultimately more rewarding. There is a cost to this of course: we in the West have got used to comfort, levels of luxury and privilege, which means that it is very difficult to live without it and this causes pain. For many of us the fact of sleeping in hostels, walking in nature all day and eating basic food, is not our normal environment and can be challenging. The need to move freely and without burden is obvious on the Camino, the simpler the better.

There is no hard and fast rule for everyone about how they should do the Camino, but generally the goal is not to punish ourselves or deprive ourselves of necessities, but to explore that area between essentials and luxuries. Choosing to stay in hotels or have a bag sent ahead can often be a very wise decision for those not as sure on their feet. Normally it is a revelation that 'I don't need as much as I thought' or 'I am so much happier with simple living and I am simply living'. This sense of freedom and a paradoxical level of happiness is what often emerges. It is a reminder of simpler times past, like the medieval pilgrims on the Camino, trusting in the generosity of others. It opens us up to other pilgrims (we are all equal on the road), fosters solidarity, and it allows us to move forward with more freedom, unencumbered by weights, pressures and externalities.

CHAPTER 17

The Joy of the Camino

All this above can all sound very intimidating and challenging, but essentially it is all about getting a level of freedom and flexibility that allows you to live in love with life, nature and others. Naturally there is a heady measure of joy that goes with that. The Camino produces some extraordinary changes and healing in people, transformations never thought possible, and this brings genuine happiness and inner peace. The process of authentically facing our fears, naming our issues and asking for divine help, does eventually deliver on its promise and the results are often miraculous. Gone is the desperate seeking of prestige and status, the frenetic accumulation of external possessions or the insatiable competitive desire to win against others. A new inner peace and sense of identity is forged that shows itself in compassion, wisdom and understanding. New ways of being emerge that are respectful of self, others and the world.

Often people come to the Camino having tried many other approaches, therapies and spiritualities, and are sometimes at their wits end. The Camino offers a level of freedom and flexibility that allows you to live lovingly, and walkers often do get some relief and satisfaction. As with most profound truths, the truth of the Camino cannot be bought, reduced to a commodity or bargained with. It demands an honest heart, a certain amount of humility and a great desire for the transcendent. Pick up your pack and walk ...

CHAPTER 18

Summary

These guidelines are an attempt to summarise the Camino experience from the standpoint of spirituality:

1   Get clear on your reason for doing the Camino, it is important to have a cause or a deep desire because when things get difficult you need an anchor to hang on to. Sometimes it will only emerge during the journey.

2   Be open to the possibility that the Spirit or a divine power is working through your experience on the Camino (this has been the case for over 1000 years); your job is to be attuned to this inner voice, trust your experience and cooperate with it as much as possible.

3   Have a short mantra or prayer that connects you with your Camino, use it to anchor your thoughts and as a reference for walking with your breath.

4   In order for you to walk the Camino you will need over 100 people to provide accommodation, food and directions for you. Get used to trusting in providence, that things will work out, that there is meaning in life's experience and that you are there for a reason.

5   Practice discovering those special moments of paradox, serendipity or kindness in your daily life, pre-Camino, by reviewing your entire day at night (the Examen, 10–15 minutes) and looking back over those moments of light, transformation or invitation were. Imagine a movie of your day where you look back at all that's happened, without judging yourself.

6   Keep a journal as an ongoing conversation with yourself of what is significant and worth remembering.

7   Get a sense of what your own ideal walking pace of rhythm is, get a sense of what this feels like so that when you are pulled off your pace you recognise it and can correct it.

8   Reduce the weight in your backpack as much as possible (ten per cent of bodyweight is a good guide), remember that this is for practical reasons (to reduce pressure on your feet and joints) but also spiritual reasons of your commitment to live a simple life, to be open to others (e.g. turn off your phone, no headphones), and to trust in providence, not your credit card.

9   Fear and anxiety are understandable obstacles to the Camino process as they promote rigidity and control; often we are unable to do much about them due to personality and habit, but what can really help is deliberately becoming aware of them, asking for healing and praying from the position of humility and weakness in asking for divine help.

10 If you are travelling with a group ensure that you get some daily solitude and quiet by walking alone for periods, agreeing to walk some stages alone, or just finding quiet places to reflect (keeping a journal is a good excuse to be alone).

11 Enjoy it and live every minute. Your faith in God and in humanity will be restored.

CHAPTER 19

Practical tips

✳ Book your basic transport in advance. If you can leave your return open, this will avoid you feeling pressured to walk further and faster than you are comfortable with to make your fixed flight home. However, booking a flight at short notice in Santiago can be very expensive. Often having a flexible ticket where you can change dates is best.

✳ Consider booking accommodation for your first night at least. Though the Camino ethic is not to book ahead, many people like to be sure of getting a bed after a long journey. Remember advance booking is possible only in private albergues or hotels.

✳ Buy quality boots or walking shoes, a rucksack and other walking equipment from an outdoor shop if you are not already a seasoned walker.

Please see the packing list below for further details.

✳ Consider buying a guide book and get one of the many Camino Apps for your phone.

✳ Consider getting a pilgrim passport in advance. The Irish Camino Society (www.caminosociety.com) supplies its own pilgrim passport.

✳ The Camino Society has an office in Dublin to ask questions or browse the bookshop or library – www.caminosociety.com. They also run many information events around the country.

✳ Nowadays virtually everything you need is available on the internet: the most popular Camino sites are www.caminosociety.com, www.caminodesantiago.me, www.csj.org.uk, and www.americanpilgrims.org. There is also a variety of commercial companies who will organise accommodation, luggage transport, food and guides if you need extra support. There is always a way to do it!

CHAPTER 20

Physical Preparation

You will want to embark on a training programme if you are not a regular and experienced walker, and make sure you have broken in your boots or walking shoes before you start your Camino. Ideally you should aim to be able to walk around twenty-five kilometres per day, though you need to be flexible depending on fitness and your goals.

CHAPTER 21

Returning from the Camino

❋ The end of the Camino Walk is only half the journey. The most important part is done at home, bringing new insight and energy to your daily life.

❋ As I experienced, it can take up to a year to really understand what has happened, such is the depth and intensity of the experience, and the slow process of understanding in the heart.

❋ There can be a terrible period of unease and discomfort on reentering 'normal' life. You have lived an extraordinary experience and there are few people that you can share it with; unfortunately people start to switch off after they've heard five minutes of Camino stories.

❋ The key challenge is integrating the valuable Camino lessons into daily life: how am I going to live differently back in my normal environment?

How can I live more simply, better connected to myself and others?

✳ It is important to find a place to think, talk and reflect about the Camino, whether that is writing about it (journaling), finding a group of others who've had the experience or connecting to one of the many online post-Camino forums.

✳ It is important to mark the significant moments and memories of the Camino with some kind of ritual or event. The use of the Camino symbols of backpack, shell and credential, can be helpful in remembering and looking forward.

✳ I recommend Alexander John Shaia's excellent book, *Returning From Camino* (2018) which deals with this often forgotten but crucial topic.